Prais  ...RATION

"John Young has provided Churches of Christ a gift by telling our history with remarkable brevity, clarity, and objectivity. This concise recounting of the beginnings of the American Restoration Movement and later developments within Churches of Christ is a great resource for Bible classes, small groups, or individuals interested in our story."

—**Garrett Best**, Minister Olive Creek Church of Christ and PhD Candidate Asbury Theological Seminary

"A very readable and well-researched history of Churches of Christ and 'the Restoration Movement' in America. Filled with interesting, historical anecdotes. An excellent read."

—**Kenny Barfield**, Headmaster Emeritus Mars Hill Bible School and former Pulpit Minister Sherrod Avenue Church of Christ

"*Visions of Restoration* is an excellent, concise work that will help Christians develop a fundamental understanding of the Restoration Movement and to see how Churches of Christ got to be where they are today. John Young expertly describes the religious environment that produced great restoration preachers of the past, as well as the issues Churches of Christ have grappled with through the years. Whether it is used in a Bible class or for personal reading, *Visions of Restoration* will be a blessing to Christians for many years to come."

—**Justin Guin**, Associate Minister Double Springs Church of Christ and Adjunct Instructor of New Testament Heritage Christian University

VISIONS OF
RESTORATION

The History of Churches of Christ

JOHN YOUNG

VISIONS OF RESTORATION
The History of Churches of Christ
Published by Cypress Publications an Imprint of Heritage Christian
University Press

Copyright © 2019 by John Young

Manufactured in the United States of America

Cataloging-in-Publication Data
John Young, 1989–
Visions of Restoration: The History of Churches of Christ / by John
Young
p. cm.
Includes index.
ISBN 978-1-7320483-4-8 (pbk.)
1. Churches of Christ—History—Textbook. I. Author.
II. Title.
BX7076 .Y68 2019 286.63007—dc20
Library of Congress Control Number: 2019941907

Cover design by Brittany McGuire
Front cover photograph, Old Mars Hill Church © Brad McKinnon
Back cover photograph, Larimore Home © Trina Ross

For information:
Cypress Publications
3625 Helton Drive
PO Box HCU
Florence, AL 35630
www.hcu.edu

For Candace,

whose love and support are indispensable

and

For my parents,

who instilled in me a love of learning.

CONTENTS

Acknowledgments / **vii**

Foreword / **xi**

1   Why Study the History of Churches of
    Christ? / **3**

2   Meet the "Big Four": Barton W. Stone, Thomas
    Campbell, Alexander Campbell and Walter
    Scott / **11**

3   The United Movement Grows / **19**

4   Challenges from the Margins / **27**

5   The Stone-Campbell Movement and the
    American Civil War / **35**

6   Dissent and Division at the Turn of the
    Twentieth Century / **43**

7   Conflict Over Premillennialism / **51**

8   The Institutionalism Debate / **59**

9   Drifting Apart Part One / **67**

10 Gainesville, Boston, and Los Angeles / **75**

11   Drifting Apart Part Two / **83**

12   The Black Church Experience / **89**

13   The History of Women Within Churches of Christ / **95**

Appendix: Resources Used and Other Suggested Readings / **103**

Index / **109**

—— ACKNOWLEDGMENTS ——

Even though this is a short book, I somehow managed to run up a fairly lengthy list of people to thank here. In no particular order...

I thank the ministers, authors, and scholars whose works inspired me to write this short introduction to the history of Churches of Christ. You should definitely check out the appendix at the end of this book, and then check out as many of their works as possible.

I thank everyone at Heritage Christian University Press/Cypress Publications for agreeing to publish this book and for going above and beyond the call of duty to make the publication process as straightforward as it can be. In particular, I thank Brad McKinnon for shepherding this project through to completion and for inviting me to tag along on an impromptu field trip with Ed Robinson to the old Mars Hill church building and Larimore Home one afternoon.

I thank the faculty and staff members of the University of Alabama Department of History, with whom I have spent over a decade, and those of Amridge

University, with whom I hope to spend many more.

I thank the staffs of the libraries where I have conducted research, either for this project or for my dissertation, during the last few years. These include the University of Alabama, the Tuscaloosa Public Library, the Florence-Lauderdale Public Library, Amridge University, Heritage Christian University, Harding School of Theology, Florida College, Freed-Hardeman University, and Beeson Divinity School.

I thank my family, especially my wife, Candace, and my parents, Vance and Robin Young. (I already dedicated this book to them, so I won't say more here.) I also thank my in-laws, Jeff and Dianna Cole, for sharing Candace with me and for welcoming me into their family. I likewise appreciate the efforts of our cats, Sherlock and Molly, who served as capable research assistants and/or paperweights for much of this project.

I thank my church family at North Tuscaloosa Church of Christ, especially the members of the college/young professionals group, who patiently sat through the first version of this material during the summer of 2018. You show this only child what Proverbs 18:24 is all about on a daily basis. I also thank the Double Springs Church of Christ, where my father-in-law, Jeff, willingly served as my guinea pig by giving this material a second test run in the spring of 2019.

Additionally, I thank the Woodlawn Church of Christ; even though I don't make it up to Florence as much as I would like, you will always feel like home to me.

Finally, I thank God, who created and who sustains me.

Any errors in what follows are mine alone unless you, the reader, want to take the heat for me.

J.Y.
Tuscaloosa, Alabama
May 2019

FOREWORD

Who are we? Where did we come from? Do we know where we are going? These are some of the important questions *Visions of Restoration: The History of Churches of Christ* seeks to answer and address. In a faith tradition that has tended to downplay its European and American historical roots, this book is extremely important. Young scholar, John Young, makes the case that church history is a "vital part of our spiritual lives."

The author grapples with various schools of thought. Are Churches of Christ merely a nineteenth-century phenomenon or did they actually begin in 33 AD and continue down to the present era? The writer argues for a balanced approach; we are indeed both a "recent phenomenon," as well as a people committed to adhering to the "ancient faith of the founders."

The writer succinctly and brilliantly traces the story of Churches of Christ in North America to its four principal leaders—Barton W. Stone (1772–1844), Thomas

Campbell (1763–1854), Walter Scott (1796–1861), and Alexander Campbell (1788–1866)—down to the issues threatening to unravel the Stone-Campbell Movement. *Visions of Restoration* surveys the Spiritism of Jesse Ferguson, the rebaptism of John Thomas, the pacifism of David Lipscomb, the Unionism of James A. Garfield, and the foreboding schism between the Disciples of Christ and Churches of Christ. Additionally, John explains the divisive and controversial issues of premillennialism, institutionalism, Crossroadsism, racism, and the role and place of women in Churches of Christ.

I am not a prophet or the son of a prophet, yet I predict that this book will prove to be very useful to the brotherhood of Churches of Christ across the United States for several reasons. First, *Visions of Restoration* fills a major void in our Sunday School and Bible class literature, as it exposes the lay and the learned alike to crucial aspects of the history of Churches of Christ. Second, students will find that this book is well-written; indeed, it is clear, concise, and instructive. Third, John takes the time to explain complicated terms, such as pre-millennial, a-millennial, and post-millennial. Fourth, the discussion questions are relevant and thought-provoking, and they will certainly generate useful dialogue and reflection. Therefore, I enthusiastically endorse this study, and I encourage congregations across the nation to consider adding it to their educational curriculum.

Edward J. Robinson
Preacher and Professor
Tyler, Texas
July 2019

VISIONS OF RESTORATION

1

WHY STUDY THE HISTORY OF CHURCHES OF CHRIST?

Readers, thank you for engaging in this study of the history of Churches of Christ—whether you're doing so voluntarily, or simply because your Bible class teacher thought that this would be a good idea. If you've never been in a study like this before, I hope that it will strengthen you in your faith as you learn more about where we came from, who we are, and indeed, *whose* we are. If you have engaged in a study like this before, and you found it dreadfully boring or irrelevant, fear not; give it a fair chance, and I think you'll come to see that church history isn't just trivia for trivia's sake, but a vital part of our spiritual lives. And if you have participated in a study like this before, and you had a great experience, hopefully you'll find that this book will address issues, individuals, and even movements that you've never heard of.

I want to say at the outset of our time together that the question of historical periodization—or, in non-historian's terms, when and where we start the story—is a surprisingly loaded one. This is especially true since we are discussing a topic which is so near and dear to our hearts. Have Churches of Christ as we know and love them today existed continuously since the events of Pentecost, as recounted in Acts 2? Or are they the product of nineteenth-century revivals, just one of many such groups born out of an atmosphere of religious innovation and creativity? Members of Churches of Christ and members of the historical profession have each, at various times, answered this question in both ways.

You may have seen the chart, frequently shared on social media, which lists the supposed start dates for various Christian fellowships. Most of the dates given are relatively recent, typically within the last three or four centuries. Only the "Church of Christ," according to this chart, began at Pentecost. Nor is this chart an exception proving the rule. In the widely read book and evangelistic tool *Muscle and a Shovel*, author Michael Shank's friend Randall claims, "Denominations are divisions from the original. The church of Christ is the original that began on the Day of Pentecost around 33 AD." Additionally, Randall states, "You see, you can't find the Catholics, the Baptists, the Methodists, the Presbyterians or the rest of them in the Bible. You can't find any of those groups by name or by practice. That's because they didn't exist in the first century."[1]

But other devout Christian believers, members of Churches of Christ, have argued that while the church was established at Pentecost, it has not existed continuously since that time, and that present-day Churches of Christ are best understood as a modern movement which seeks to restore, or return, Christianity to the teachings and practices of the first-century church. Many historians, including some who are members of Churches of Christ, have taken just such an approach. But this understanding isn't just the province of scholars. In fact, the noted evangelist Walter Scott was so strongly convinced that the long-lost church had been restored in his lifetime that he affixed a specific date to the preaching of what he believed to be the first full gospel sermon in nearly two millennia! (By the way, Scott was the man who developed the five-fingers-for-five-steps-of-salvation memory device.)

Both answers have their potential strengths and weaknesses. The notion that Churches of Christ began in 33 AD and have existed down to this day is appealing because it seeks to connect us directly with those whose faith we hope to imitate. However, there are a couple of

1. Michael Shank, *Muscle and a Shovel*, 2nd ed. (Lightning Source Press, 2013), 222–223.

issues, not always readily apparent, which arise when we just assume that there is a historical connection. First, claiming (or at least implying) that Churches of Christ have existed continuously since the first century doesn't sit well with our simultaneous claim to be restoring, or to have restored, teachings and practices which had been overlooked previously. More simply: if the Church of Christ has always existed, then what exactly are we restoring, or what exactly have we restored? And second, those who look for possible Churches of Christ scattered throughout the last two thousand years of Christian history are correct when they say that we are not the first people to try to restore the faith of the first century church. But in practice, they sometimes ignore very important differences between what we do today and what some of these earlier restorers did in their lifetimes.

For instance, in 1645, the Puritan minister John Cotton published a book titled *The Way of the Churches of Christ in New England.* At first glance, this might seem to be a useful source for a class such as ours. Modern members of Churches of Christ might find themselves nodding in agreement with the book's opening line, which affirms that Christ "in his Gospel hath instituted" his church, or with Cotton's second proposition, which commands Christians to "join themselves ... to some one or other such a particular visible Church of Christ."

They would probably be less excited about Cotton's acknowledgment that "we all who are borne in Christian Churches, are baptized in our infancy."[2]

Yet the other answer—that Churches of Christ are only a nineteenth-century (or later) phenomenon—has its issues, too. For one, to say that Churches of Christ are totally a product of the 1800s is to run the risk of cutting ourselves off from earlier generations of believers who sought the same goal that we seek. Even if we don't always hold the exact same views on certain doctrinal or practical matters, these earlier movements have often set the stage for our own efforts. One powerful example can even be found in the theology of Barton W. Stone, one of the key restorers of the early nineteenth century. Stone, and many of those associated with him, believed strongly in the reality of miraculous and ecstatic demonstrations of the power of the Holy Spirit within the individual believer. Yet even though this belief is not widely shared among Churches of Christ today, other aspects of Stone's teachings—his preference for the name "Church of Christ," for instance—have had considerable impact on our predecessors' efforts to be like the first century church.

---

2. John Cotton, *The Way of the Churches of Christ in New England* (1645; repr., Weston Rhyn, UK: Quinta Press, 2008), 5–9.

So, how do I—as a historian, a minister, and a believer—answer the question? I believe that Christ's church was established at Pentecost, as we read about in Acts 2. I believe that we have a divinely-inspired record of many of its activities, as well as select letters and other writings from its earliest decades, given to us by God for our instruction.

I also believe, however, that the church gradually drifted away from its original mission. I believe that, throughout the course of Christian history, a number of individuals and movements arose which tried to refocus the church on its original tasks, using the example of the first-century church as a pattern. And I believe that modern Churches of Christ (and the wider restoration movement they are historically connected to) represent one of the most recent, and perhaps the most thorough, of these movements.

In short, I believe that we are both a recent phenomenon and a people who authentically seek to emulate the ancient faith of the founders. I believe that while we have made great strides along the path of restoration, the process is not yet fully complete, if it ever can be completed. And I believe that we can't afford to lose sight of our goal and become complacent with where we are and what we have.

What do you believe?

Discussion Questions

1. What are your past experiences with the study of church history? Have you ever had a class on the history of Churches of Christ before? If so, did you find it helpful or interesting? (Be honest!)

2. Why is the question of when Churches of Christ began such a difficult question to answer? What are the larger possible implications of the different answers?

3. Have you ever thought about historical study as part of a healthy spiritual life? Why or why not?

— 2 —
MEET THE "BIG FOUR":
BARTON W. STONE, THOMAS CAMPBELL,
ALEXANDER CAMPBELL & WALTER SCOTT

We in the United States likely give little thought to the First Amendment's two religious clauses during a typical day. We are generally free to practice our faith as we wish, and we are generally free from government-established religion. But this is only a relatively recent development in human history, and in some places around the world, religious freedoms are not guaranteed even today. So for early inhabitants of the United States, the First Amendment was something to be cherished and, just as importantly, its protections were to be exercised on a regular basis. As Americans moved westward in the late eighteenth and early nineteenth centuries, the Christian faith spread along with them. Though there had been official religions in several of the colonies, the territories were truly a religious marketplace, with a variety of new or growing Christian denominations, such as Baptists, Methodists, and to a lesser extent Presbyterians, rushing in. Church membership rates rose dramatically during these first decades of the nineteenth century, going from roughly one-sixth of the population in 1776 to about one-third in 1850.

But competition for conversions was fierce, and the appearance of new churches was common. Pushing back against this dangerous tendency toward division, some Christians sought to unify different strands of Christianity by creating interdenominational institutions such as the American Bible Society. These types of organizations gave members of varied Christian traditions a shared goal, vision, or task—for the ABS, the printing and distribution of the Bible—which would lessen the emphasis on the doctrinal distinctions which divided them. Others, however, sought to do away with denominational identity altogether by, they believed, jettisoning nearly two thousand years of accumulated tradition and returning to the faith of the first century.

Often differing as much from each other as they did the denominations they left, such leaders nevertheless shared a common goal: "They aimed to be restorers and not reformers."[3] Restoration movements popped up in a variety of places throughout the United States. Abner Jones and Elias Smith tried to be "Christians only" up in New England, while James O'Kelly did the same in Virginia. Even Joseph Smith of the Latter-day Saints was a restorationist in some sense, though the exact nature of what he and his followers sought to bring back was remarkably different. Four of these early restorers in particular proved to be the most important for the long-term history and development of Churches of Christ: the aforementioned Barton W. Stone and Walter Scott, along with father and son duo Thomas Campbell and Alexander Campbell.

Stone was born in 1772 and spent his earliest years in Maryland and Virginia. Baptized as an infant into the Church of England, which was the established church in Maryland, Stone was generally apathetic or even opposed to religion as a young man because of the controversies which divided Christians from one another. Even so, Stone eventually converted to Presbyterianism and became a clergyman. Moving to Kentucky in 1796, he was a participant in a massive series of revivals held at Cane Ridge in 1801.

3. Lars P. Qualben, *A History of the Christian Church*, rev. ed. (New York: Thomas Nelson and Sons, 1958), 568.

These revivals brought together Christians from a variety of denominations. But this ecumenism put Stone at risk of angering his employers in the Presbyterian Church. In 1803, he and several likeminded preachers, who shared his distrust of Calvinist teachings on total depravity and unconditional election, were expelled from the Synod of Kentucky. These men united into an unofficial "Springfield Presbytery" for a short time, but in 1804, they dissolved even this small governing body in favor of congregational rule. Over the following decades, Stone continued working throughout Kentucky, preaching in favor of adult immersion and against the sprinkling of infants. Other important themes of his preaching included his rejection of religious tradition and his disavowal of participation in politics. Stone also shared these beliefs through a newspaper, the *Christian Messenger*, for nearly two decades. By 1830, those influenced by Stone—scattered chiefly throughout Kentucky, Ohio, and Tennessee—numbered approximately 15,000.

The stories of the other three members of the "Big Four"—Thomas Campbell, his son Alexander, and Walter Scott—were in some ways more closely linked. Thomas Campbell was born in Ireland in 1763. A Presbyterian like Stone, Campbell also felt called to ministry, and in 1807, he traveled to the United States, where he received a commission to preach in western Pennsylvania. Yet his belief that communion should be open, not restricted to church members, ran contrary to church teachings, and in 1808, the Synod of North America suspended him. Just as Stone had done a few years earlier, Campbell and his associates formed a smaller organization called the Christian Association of Washington which brought together a variety of non-conformists from several Christian groups.

Thomas's son Alexander joined him in the U.S. that same year. Originally fearful that he and his father would sharply disagree on religious matters—Alexander had himself taken up the cause of restoration in the time since his father left Europe—he found instead a strong ally and the beginnings of a restoration movement. In these early years, the Campbells found some common ground with local Baptists, and the younger Campbell even edited a newspaper titled the *Christian Baptist.* In this and other publications, he argued for a "restoration of the ancient order of things."[4] This restoration, in Campbell's view, would help bring about Jesus' return to Earth and the onset of the millennium.

4. David Edwin Harrell Jr., *A Social History of the Disciples of Christ* (Tuscaloosa, AL: The University of Alabama Press, 2003), 1:7.

Walter Scott, the last of our "Big Four," immigrated to the United States in 1818, a few years after the Campbells made their respective passages. While in the city of Pittsburgh, Scott came into contact with a small restorationist group led by George Forrester, who had been influenced by teachings similar to those which had shaped young Alexander Campbell. (It was in the home of another influential restorationist, Robert Richardson, that Scott first actually met the younger Campbell.)

Like Alexander Campbell, Scott was fully committed to the notion that the complete restoration of Christ's church would bring about his return to Earth and the beginning of the millennium. Scott also, as noted earlier, believed that the beginnings of that very restoration had taken place in his lifetime—in his own preaching, no less. Working in the Western Reserve, Scott made another important contribution to later Churches of Christ when he codified a "plan of salvation" which included six steps: belief, repentance, baptism, forgiveness, the gift of the Holy Spirit, and the receiving of eternal life. Scott later condensed these six steps into five, matching the number of fingers on the human hand, by subsuming eternal life under the gift of the Holy Spirit. (Later generations would remove forgiveness and the Holy Spirit from the mnemonic, adding hearing and confession to keep the tally at five.)

With four of the most important early restorers introduced, we'll draw the chapter to a close. Next chapter, we will see that many of those associated with Stone's movement, as well as those affiliated with the Campbells and Scott, eventually joined together under a united banner of restorationism. Yet we will also see how theological, geographical, and socioeconomic differences threatened to unravel the movement before it fully got off the ground.

Discussion Questions

1. Had you heard of Stone, the Campbells, and/or Scott before? If so, what did you know about them previously?

2. What beliefs do you share in common with these men? Where do your beliefs differ from theirs?

3. What do you think it means to restore first-century Christianity in the present day?

3

THE UNITED MOVEMENT GROWS

In our last chapter, we introduced the four individuals who proved to be most significant in the history of Churches of Christ in the early nineteenth century: Barton W. Stone, Thomas Campbell, his son Alexander Campbell, and Walter Scott. Now, we will look at the story of how these men's efforts to restore the New Testament church came together into a relatively unified movement, leading to rapid growth in the run-up to and through the American Civil War.

The first few decades of the nineteenth century witnessed significant religious innovation and competition throughout the United States. While some moved in markedly new directions, including Transcendentalists like Ralph Waldo Emerson and Henry David Thoreau, others sought the equally radical goal of restoring the first century church in the present. The boundaries between these kinds of restoration movements and the denominations from which they sprang were not always clear. As we saw in the last chapter, Stone's movement first took some tentative steps away from the Presbyterian Church before making a clean break, and the Campbells' Christian Association of Washington maintained ties with Baptist churches for a significant period of time because of a shared commitment to adult baptism by immersion.

It can also be difficult to untangle the various threads of restorationism which were brought together in the united movement, especially in these early decades. Over time, the more conservative congregations, which were also more likely to be poorer, rural, and southern, gradually came to prefer the name "Churches of Christ," whereas their wealthier, more liberal, urban, northern brethren opted for "Disciples of Christ" or "Christian Churches." Even so, these dividing lines were not absolute, and the terms were more or less interchangeable for much of the nineteenth century.

Further adding to the confusion, restorers often came to very different conclusions about how to interpret scripture—not just over relatively small matters, but over fundamental issues such as whether converts from other Christian denominations needed to be rebaptized or the existence of miraculous manifestations of the Holy Spirit's power in the present age. However, these men and women had at least one thing in common:

their goal to restore the ancient order in the modern age.

Accordingly, prominent figures in the Stone and Campbell movements sought in 1832 to join their efforts together. The process of unification was not totally smooth; some of those associated with Stone felt they had less in common with Campbell, and they decided to cast their lots with the followers of another restorationist, James O'Kelly. But broadly speaking, the two movements merged at the national level and at the local level, with congregations in some places uniting into one church, while those in other communities simply acknowledged each another as faithful Christians.

According to one estimate, this combined Stone-Campbell Movement (also known as the American Restoration Movement or as the Restoration Movement) was the fastest-growing Christian body in the nation during the 1850s; indeed, based on the results of the 1870 census, it was the fifth-largest Christian group in the United States. Though not the only reason for the movement's growth, the increased national prominence of movement leaders did play a significant role. This was particularly true when Alexander Campbell engaged in two high-profile debates—one with freethinker Robert Owen in 1829, the other with Catholic bishop John Purcell in 1837—which caught the attention of much of the wider American religious world.

But there were some cracks in the foundation. Two of the most important debates in the antebellum restoration churches revolved around (1) the use of instrumental music in worship and (2) the creation of extra-congregational societies to coordinate and undertake mission work. These disagreements were undoubtedly doctrinal in nature, but they were also indicative of other fissures within the movement which went beyond opinions on specific theological issues—geographic location, socioeconomic status, the rural-urban divide, and competing hermeneutical approaches to scripture would all eventually factor into the arguments over instruments and societies, as we will see in future chapters.

Though instrumental music would not become a dividing issue until well after the close of the Civil War, heated debate about the practice began as early as the 1850s, especially in the state of Kentucky. Advocates argued, for instance, that movement churches could not appeal to potential converts without instrumental worship. And at first, opponents criticized the introduction of instruments not primarily on theological grounds, but on cultural and economic ones. For example, Benjamin Franklin (not the Founding Father, but the restorationist preacher) criticized the use of the organ as a frivolous attempt to fit into "*fashionable society*" by "*refined* gentlemen [who] have *refined ears*, enjoy fine music manufactured for French theaters, interspersed with *short* prayers and *very short* sermons."[5]

A major turning point was reached in 1860 when the congregation in Midway, Kentucky became the first (or at least the first for which we have record) to introduce an instrument into its worship services. According to one observer, the melodeon was added in large part to cover up the congregation's poor singing, which could "scare even the rats from worship."[6] The move was controversial, however, even within the congregation. One evening, a dissenting elder boosted one of his slaves up to and through a window and had him push the instrument out the window before escaping with it. (A replacement was brought in shortly thereafter.) Other critics, including Moses Lard, began to speak out against the practice on theological grounds in the aftermath of the Midway incident. Yet at this point, the practice did not lead to the permanent division of the movement.

5. Benjamin Franklin, "Instrumental Music in Churches," *American Christian Review*, January 31, 1860, 18. Quoted in Richard T. Hughes, *Reviving the Ancient Faith: The Story of Churches of Christ in America* (Grand Rapids, MI: Eerdmans, 1996), 86.

6. L.L. Pinkerton, "Instrumental Music in Churches," *American Christian Review*, February 28, 1860, 34. Quoted in Earl Irvin West, *The Search for the Ancient Order: A History of the Restoration Movement* (Germantown, TN: Religious Book Service, 1949–1987), 1:311.

Another significant issue in the antebellum movement was the missionary society. One of the major religious developments during the last decades of the eighteenth century and first decades of the nineteenth, as we have mentioned previously, was the creation of interdenominational organizations which sought to bring believers from a variety of backgrounds together in pursuit of a shared goal, such as mission work or the printing and distribution of Bibles. Many early restorationists criticized such organizations on the grounds that these organizations supplanted the individual congregation and threatened its God-given authority. As time went on, however, other restorationists began to informally coordinate mission and charity efforts across congregations.

The American Christian Missionary Society, the first official movement-wide organization, appeared in 1849. The ACMS sought to coordinate and finance evangelistic efforts on the basis of expediency; God had given the command to preach, supporters argued, but no specific blueprint for how to accomplish the task. While there was general consensus that evangelism was a wholly appropriate goal, the ACMS was a point of great contention because, to many, it seemed to go against biblical teachings on congregational autonomy. Leading restorationist figures came out both for and against the society; Alexander Campbell ultimately supported the

ACMS, while David Lipscomb, Tolbert Fanning, and others led the opposition.

For all of the ink and paper devoted to the society question, though, the movement held together for the moment.

Discussion Questions

1. Do you agree or disagree that the goal of trying to restore first-century Christianity in the present day is radical? Why?

2. In what ways did the divisive issues within the antebellum restoration churches mirror those within Churches of Christ today? In what ways did they differ?

3. Why do you think that the use of instrumental music and the creation of the ACMS did not immediately lead to a formal split within the restoration churches? Was this the right response? How does it differ from later instances of disagreement?

4

CHALLENGES FROM THE MARGINS

The last chapter ended, you may remember, on a relatively high note. While the antebellum movement to restore the early church was threatened by disagreements over the use of instruments in worship and over support for the American Christian Missionary Society, believers largely remained united in their pursuit of the first-century faith—a goal that all parties involved shared, though they disagreed on a number of theological and practical matters.

Controversy also arose in other corners of the movement, however, and the beliefs of two ministers in particular went beyond the limits of fellowship and tolerance. Though neither minister is exactly a household name today, their stories are still important to us for what they reveal about the movement's history before the Civil War. First, the two men's highly unorthodox teachings help illustrate the broad range of religious beliefs held by Americans during the first half of the nineteenth century; and second, they show us that while the early restorers were wholly committed to seeking the unification of all Christians into one church, there were still core theological tenets that they could not abandon in good conscience, even in pursuit of Christian fellowship.

Jesse B. Ferguson

In 1854, Jesse B. Ferguson, the minister of the Church of Christ in Nashville, Tennessee, shocked more than a few people when he claimed to have had contact with the spirits of the deceased. Ferguson had led the Nashville congregation since 1846, and he had brought a solid reputation and considerable talent to the job. Under Ferguson's watch, the church had grown at a noticeable clip. Too, he contributed regularly to multiple religious newspapers, making him a well-known figure within the larger movement.

Early in his tenure, however, Ferguson courted controversy when he published an article in *Christian Magazine* on the doctrine of the "harrowing of Hell." While the teaching (based on 1 Peter 3:18–4:6) that Jesus descended into the realm of the deceased between his crucifixion and resurrection to proclaim his victory over sin and death is fairly commonplace in the wider Christian world, Ferguson's adherence to the doctrine ruffled many feathers, including those of Alexander Campbell and Samuel Church. Church, in fact, wrote in response to the article that Ferguson apparently had "a maggot in his brain."[7] Ferguson's later claims about having contacted the dead proved even more controversial, provoking Alexander Campbell himself to visit the congregation to try to restore order. Ferguson ultimately resigned from his position in 1856, leaving a highly fractured church in his wake.

John Thomas

Jesse B. Ferguson was not the only antebellum restorationist to take a sharp turn and find himself outside of the movement's good graces. Roughly two decades earlier, an English doctor named John Thomas had caused a similar stir and likewise provoked the wrath of Alexander Campbell. Thomas, as a young man, had crossed the Atlantic Ocean in search of gainful employment. Thinking that he was about to die in a shipwreck, he pledged his life to ministry (if God would spare it) and soon came into contact with restorationists upon his arrival in North America. Thomas was an enthusiastic

7. Alexander Campbell, "The Spirits in Prison," *Millennial Harbinger* Fourth Series 2, no. 7 (July 1852): 414. Quoted in West, *The Search for the Ancient Order,* 1:264.

convert, preaching fervently in and around Richmond, Virginia, and editing a religious newspaper called the *Apostolic Advocate*.

But Thomas came to diverge from the theological core of the movement in a number of ways. For instance, he was an annihilationist, believing and teaching that the souls of the unsaved would be permanently destroyed rather than tormented eternally in Hell. He also devoted a great deal of time and energy to interpreting contemporary events in light of biblical end-times prophecies. Yet oddly enough, the issue that led Thomas to formally break with the larger restoration movement (and vice versa) was the rebaptism of converts from other Christian traditions. Thomas believed it was necessary; Alexander Campbell and the majority of those associated with him did not. The two men ultimately cut ties with one another after a period of heated debate and went their separate ways. (There is, of course, a certain irony in the fact that the disfellowshipped Thomas's position eventually became the dominant view in many Churches of Christ.)

Despite the controversy, John Thomas continued to write and to preach along the eastern seaboard and in his homeland throughout the rest of his life. His movement achieved its greatest successes in the British city of Birmingham and in Richmond, Virginia. During the American Civil War, his followers took on the name

"Christadelphians"—a word meaning "brethren in Christ"—so that they could seek conscientious objector status. Holding in high regard Thomas's writings, especially his prophetic work *Elpis Israel*, modern-day Christadelphians continue to preach a distinctive version of Christianity that combines the restorationism of a Stone or a Campbell with the end-times fascinations of groups like the Seventh-day Adventists.

Conclusion

Why should we care about Jesse B. Ferguson and John Thomas more than a century and a half later? After all, their followers never amounted to more than a small fraction of the movement to restore the early church, even in their respective heydays. Too, Ferguson's teachings spawned no lasting group, and Thomas's Christadelphian movement numbers only in the tens of thousands of adherents worldwide today.

Nevertheless, Ferguson and Thomas remind us that the history of Churches of Christ is filled with twists and turns and an unusual cast of characters. The teachings espoused by the two men and their followers represented real challenges to the beliefs of their fellow restorationists, even if those teachings were unlikely to become orthodoxy within the movement. Believers had to make tough decisions about how far, exactly, the bounds of Christian fellowship and unity could extend. In some cases, as we have seen, a common goal (such as the restoration of first-century Christianity) could smooth over fairly significant theological divisions. In other situations, however, those disagreements proved too severe.

As we will see in our next chapter, the single greatest challenge to unity within the restoration churches came not from an instrument or from a missionary society or from a wayward minister but from the American Civil War itself. Many American Christian groups, in fact, would be permanently split by the conflict and the political issues that led to it. Between 1836 and 1845, the Presbyterian, Baptist, and Methodist churches all divided along geographical lines over the issue of slavery, presaging the division of the country as a whole during the Civil War. (Of the three groups, only the Methodist Church would later reunite.)

The conventional wisdom within many present-day Churches of Christ is that our fellowship did not split during the Civil War, as so many other Christian groups did. There is an element of truth in this notion, but the view is also somewhat misleading—or, at least, incomplete. Although there was no lasting formal split among the restoration churches as a direct result of the war, the conflict did exacerbate the theological and personal divisions that we have previously mentioned. These fault lines would eventually rupture into full-blown separation. But that's a story for the next chapter.

Discussion Questions

1. Had you heard of either Jesse B. Ferguson or John Thomas before reading this chapter? If so, in what context? If not, why do you think that might be the case?

2. Why is it important to be aware of and understand the different paths taken by various restorationists from past generations, even if we might not necessarily agree with all of their beliefs?

3. Do you think the congregational polity of Churches of Christ (i.e., not having any official institutions above the level of the individual congregation) makes it easier for individual ministers to influence their congregations, either for good or for ill? Why or why not?

— 5 —

THE STONE-CAMPBELL MOVEMENT AND
THE AMERICAN CIVIL WAR

As we mentioned at the end of the previous chapter, the American Civil War posed an enormous threat to the unity of the restorationists around the middle of the nineteenth century; in fact, many other Christian groups had already divided as a result of the issues, chiefly slavery, that led to the war. But while the restoration churches themselves did not formally split during this period, the conflict undoubtedly watered the seeds of division which had already been planted during the antebellum period. For instance, the American Christian Missionary Society—the existence of which had been a source of controversy in and of itself—angered many southern restorationists in 1863 when its leaders passed a resolution of support for the Union cause.

Perhaps more substantively, the Civil War revealed a tension between those who believed that a full restoration of New Testament Christianity necessarily included the refusal to use violence, on the one hand, and those who believed that the movement's members ought to be involved in military and governmental service on the other. Well-known figures found themselves on opposite sides of the issue. One anecdote holds that a Confederate soldier attended services at David Lipscomb's Nashville congregation to determine whether the message preached was sufficiently pro-Confederate. According to the story, the soldier later reported to his commanding officer that "I have not reached a conclusion as to whether or not the doctrine of the sermon is loyal to the Southern Confederacy, but I am profoundly convinced that he is loyal to the Christian religion."[8] (Lipscomb, like many of his fellow believers, was a pacifist.)

Other disciples, however, believed that military service was perfectly acceptable. The most notable of this group was future U.S. president James A. Garfield of Ohio, who rose to the rank of major general in the Union Army during the war. Garfield would transition seamlessly from his military service into a seat in the

8. F.D. Srygley, *Biographies and Sermons* (1898; repr., Nashville: Gospel Advocate, 1961), 161.

House of Representatives, where he stayed until the start of his brief presidency. (We will devote more attention to Garfield in the next chapter.)

Though the American Civil War and its related issues did not lead to an official, permanent division of the restoration churches, there was at least one other major change brought about by the conflict. The war years led to an increased sense of sectional rivalry between northern and southern churches, with churches in a given region increasingly giving their support to colleges and church newspapers in that same region. Such a division would make it difficult for unity-minded leaders in the postwar era to keep the movement's churches all facing the same direction.

Another key development from the 1860s was the death of Alexander Campbell in 1866. While Campbell was hardly the only influential figure in the restoration churches during his lifetime—there were plenty of people who disagreed with him on a host of issues—his passing was nevertheless emblematic of a much larger changing of the guard. The new generation of leaders that rose to prominence in the postbellum world would be less inclined to compromise, less inclined to seek unity despite diversity in practices, than the one which had preceded it.

The year of Campbell's death also saw a number of prominent restorationists establishing new papers or revitalizing old ones. Many of these editors and authors would use their publications to draw lines in the sand, so to speak, in the battle over missionary societies. Ben Franklin (again, the preacher, not the Founding Father) wielded his *American Christian Review* as a leading critic of the societies, while David Lipscomb's rebooted *Gospel Advocate* became the most prominent paper among southern churches. Additionally, Isaac Errett began a new periodical, the *Christian Standard*, in which he championed the cause of the missionary society.

The ACMS was a particular point of contention along sectional lines, in no small part because the organization—the only national body among restoration churches at that time—had taken a Unionist stance during the Civil War. Opponents of the society, many (though certainly not all) of them southerners, argued that the society illegitimately supplanted the church's role in evangelism and that its existence implied that the church was incapable of fulfilling the Great Commission. Defenders, however, claimed that the church had been given the task of evangelism, but no specific method to follow, meaning that Christians could use whatever means were most appropriate or "expedient." They also pointed out that some of the strongest opponents of the ACMS were founders and boosters of Christian schools and newspapers. If those institutions were permissible, they asked, then why not the missionary society?

Predictably, the use of instrumental music in worship was another major fault line among restorationists in the latter half of the nineteenth century. Even though relatively few congregations opted to use instruments—one 1868 estimate posited that fewer than fifty out of two thousand churches had done so—many of the ones which had taken that step were prominent churches in large cities. Notable figures like Isaac Errett saw the addition of instrumental music as a matter of opinion, or of expediency. Even though Errett himself was personally opposed to the practice, he cautioned others not to see it as a dividing issue. But division was not so easily avoided. For instance, the church in Springfield, Missouri voted in early 1886 by nearly a two-to-one margin to use an organ in worship. The relationship between those in favor and those opposed fractured in the months following, with a worship service in January 1887 devolving into chaos. At one point, the congregation's organist drowned out a critic by playing over him, and the two factions each tried to sing different songs at the same time.

Lest it seem like these were the only two important issues, we also need to take stock of the different ways in which restoration churches interacted with the society around them. In broadest terms, members of the churches living in urban settings, typically more well-to-do and further north, believed that the best way for the church to accomplish its mission was for it to be a societally respectable institution. In addition to (generally) providing greater support to missionary societies and being more likely to include instrumental worship, these believers were also more likely to support higher education and to desire for their leaders to have some measure of formal academic training. For instance, a "Disciples Divinity House," an organization for students from the group, was established at the prestigious University of Chicago in 1894. Their counterparts in rural, southern, less well-to-do congregations offered a different view of the proper relationship between church and society. "The Bible truths were static," Earl West writes while summarizing this view, "the Bible teaching the same thing in 1885 that it had taught in 1845, and any attempt to change the church to alter the laws of God to conform with the changing environmental factors in society [was to be] considered objectionable."[9]

One powerful example of how all of these factors came together was the presidential campaign of James A. Garfield. Garfield's presidency would not last long, of course; he was shot by a disgruntled job seeker in July

9. West, *The Search for the Ancient Order*, 2:177–178.

1881 and languished for a couple of months before dying in September of that year. Yet his political career, as we will see in the following chapter, was a flashpoint for many of the controversies that had plagued the movement throughout the nineteenth century.

Discussion Questions

1. Before this chapter, did you know that many of the early restorationists were pacifists? Has that stance changed or diminished over time?

2. To what extent are Churches of Christ still divided along geographic lines today? What colleges, newspapers, or other institutions is your congregation most closely connected with, and where are these things located?

3. What do you know about James Garfield at this point? Were you aware that he was a notable restoration figure in addition to being a U.S. president?

—————————— 6 ——————————

DISSENT AND DIVISION AT THE TURN OF THE TWENTIETH CENTURY

The last chapter ended with a brief mention of James A. Garfield, an Ohio restorationist who was chosen by the American people to become President of the United States in the election of 1880. As we noted then, Garfield's campaign and short presidency stirred up quite a bit of controversy within the movement, and opinion was largely split across sectional lines. Although his political career did not directly bring about the official division within the restoration churches—a division that the U.S. Census Bureau would acknowledge in 1906—it certainly revealed the theological, political, and geographical tensions that were bubbling up to the surface during this period.

Garfield carried no southern states in the election of 1880. Northern opinion was much more favorable, however, with John F. Rowe of the *American Christian*

Review opining that "we think our brethren at large feel pleased that so distinguished an honor has been conferred on one of our brethren."[10]   Garfield's inauguration, presidency, and patience through the final months of his life brought a great amount of publicity and prestige to the Disciples, particularly in the North. Southern restorationists were less enthused. David Lipscomb led the way, pointing out that during the war, both Union and Confederate soldiers had relied on Romans 13 to justify their submission to political authority, leading fellow Christians to kill one another. He also noted, somewhat uncharitably, that if God had lifted Garfield to the presidency for a purpose—a common claim among his supporters—then he must have had some purpose for allowing him to be assassinated as well.

The Division Is Officially Recognized

Jumping forward a quarter of a century, the 1906 U.S. Census of Religious Bodies provided the first official

10. John F. Rowe, "General Garfield's Nomination," *American Christian Review,* July 10, 1880, 186. Quoted in Jerry Rushford, "Political Disciple: The Relationship Between James A. Garfield and the Disciples of Christ" (PhD diss., University of California at Santa Barbara, 1977), 262.

.

recognition of a fact that had been true for some time already: the restoration churches were no longer one body but two. Yet 1906 was not the beginning, but rather the culmination, of a much longer process of division along the various theological, political, and geographical fault lines we have discussed so far. Even at the beginning of this restoration movement, there had never been complete unity on all matters—including, as we have seen, some very substantial issues. But there had been a sense, shared by many, that unity was at least as important as restoration. In other words, many believed that uniting all Christians into one fellowship, even if they disagreed on some matters, was just as important as restoring the faith of the first century. This sentiment would come to be much more prevalent in the group now known as the Disciples of Christ, while its converse—the belief that a restoration of the particulars of the early church is the only possible basis for unity—became a more common belief among Churches of Christ.

The long-running debate regarding the proper name, or names, for the church reveals much about the final division that eventually ensued in the late nineteenth and early twentieth centuries. From the outset of the movement, there had been disagreement, or at least difference of opinion, over that question. Throughout much of the nineteenth century, terms like "Church of

Christ," "Christian Church," and "Disciples of Christ" were used as synonyms by many. Yet as far back as the 1820s, Barton W. Stone advocated for the exclusive use of "Churches of Christ" as a description of local congregations, while Campbell preferred "Disciples" instead. In fact, by the 1840s, "Churches of Christ" had become the "standard designation" for southern churches, as historian Richard T. Hughes has noted.[11] And even though the two subgroups maintained connections and shared many common goals, they began to drift further and further apart over the issues they emphasized. Churches of Christ (as a whole) were more concerned with restoring the early church, while the Disciples (as a whole) gave greater priority to the unification of all Christian believers. This categorization is oversimplified, to be sure, but it generally conveys the growing-apart that occurred in the latter half of the nineteenth century.

In 1906, the Census Director contacted David Lipscomb, editor of the *Gospel Advocate*, to ask whether "Churches of Christ" and "Disciples of Christ" were still one and the same body. Lipscomb replied in the negative, acknowledging the reality that the movement had already come apart. From that point forward, Churches of Christ and Disciples of Christ have been recognized

---

11. Hughes, *Reviving the Ancient Faith,* 16–17.

as two separate groups, and the two churches have embarked on remarkably different paths since then. The division recognized by the U.S. Census Bureau was hardly an even split in terms of raw numbers. Even though the membership statistics from 1906, which listed the Disciples at just under a million members and Churches of Christ at just over 150,000, are suspect, Churches of Christ were still a distinct minority in the 1916 religious census a decade later.

Was there another possible outcome? Or were the divisions too large to overcome? It is hard to say. Certainly, there were practical matters that made unity difficult; for instance, a single worship service could not be instrumental and a cappella at the same time, as Earl West has pointed out.[12] Other dividing lines were equally stark. Southern restorationists, particularly in the postwar period, frequently criticized their northern brethren for spending money building nicer buildings and adding instruments to their worship services instead of devoting the money to charity work.

But there were also individuals who sought to bridge the gap between the two wings of the movement, none more prominent than Tennessee native Theophilus Brown (T.B.) Larimore. Larimore was personally opposed to the use of instruments in worship, yet he

12. West, *The Search for the Ancient Order*, 2:446–447.

refused to engage in debates over the practice because he felt that doing so distracted from the ultimate mission of the church: the proclamation of Jesus Christ. This stance made him the target of much criticism; many on both sides of the issue tried to win him over and criticized him when he did not relent. The leader of the Nashville Bible School reportedly forbade Larimore from speaking at the school because of his position, for instance. Yet Larimore stuck to his guns, refusing to condemn his fellow believers and accepting invitations to speak from both sides of the aisle. "They may refuse to recognize or fellowship or affiliate with ME," he wrote, "but I will NEVER refuse to recognize or fellowship or affiliate with them— NEVER."[13] Whether or not division was the only "correct" response is a matter for a different book. But there was another option.

In our next chapter, we will cover an early twentieth century controversy within Churches of Christ regarding teachings about the millennium—a conflict with significant implications for our fellowship today, particularly in the realms of eschatology and conflict resolution, yet one many modern members are almost

13. T.B. Larimore, "Reply to O.P. Spiegel's Open Letter," *Christian Standard* (July 24, 1897): 965–967. Quoted in D. Newell Williams, Douglas A. Foster, and Paul M. Bowers, eds., *The Stone-Campbell Movement: A Global History* (St. Louis: Chalice Press, 2013), 93.

entirely unfamiliar with.

Discussion Questions

1. Why was the presidential campaign of James A. Garfield so controversial? Are there any lessons for modern Christians to learn about the relationship between the church and politics?

2. What does the debate over the proper name (or names) for the church reveal about the underlying divisions within the nineteenth-century movement? What do you believe are the proper names for the church?

3. Was the division between Disciples of Christ and Churches of Christ inevitable? Was it possible or desirable to maintain unity despite the many differences between the two groups?

7

CONFLICT OVER PREMILLENNIALISM

The 1906 religious census, you may remember from the previous chapter, brought belated recognition to an important development that had come to pass during the previous few decades: the separation of the Disciples of Christ and the Churches of Christ into two separate religious bodies. From here on, our story will stick almost exclusively to historical developments within Churches of Christ, with attention given to some of the smaller fellowships which separated themselves from the larger group in the following decades over a number of theological issues.

In this chapter, we will see Churches of Christ again being tested by division within the first half of the twentieth century—this time, over the hot-button issue of premillennialism. While the contours of this split are less well known to most believers today, the conflict did a great deal to delineate the movement's eschatology (beliefs about the end times) and the methods that would be used to settle future disputes.

The post-World War One period found Churches of Christ, as a whole, increasingly involved in mission work, building and rebuilding congregations domestically and across the globe. There were, of course, divisions and disagreements within the movement—even during this era, which is sometimes thought to be a "golden age" in the history of Churches of Christ. Yet these debates, as heated as they could be, often helped believers evaluate and reevaluate their beliefs in pursuit of the standard of the first-century church. While the issues that were litigated through this process may seem of relatively minor import to some, for others, these apparently insignificant topics could be of the greatest importance. For all of the issues which arose in Churches of Christ during the early decades of the twentieth century, however, only the group of congregations which use one cup for the Lord's Supper, and the group which does not have Sunday School classes, sought to fully separate themselves from the larger body of Churches of Christ. A shared commitment to restorationism kept the movement largely united despite other differences of opinion. Not until controversy over a subject known as "dispensational premillennialism" arose were the bonds of fellowship again pushed beyond their breaking point.

Before we proceed with that story, however, we need to briefly define some terms. There are a number of words ending in "-millennialism" that characterize different theological positions about Revelation 20:4–6. Postmillennialism, a viewpoint shared by many in the early nineteenth century, including Alexander Campbell, holds that human progress, perhaps including the restoration of the church and the unification of all believers, would bring about the *millennium*, and that Jesus would return to the Earth *after* that time (hence, *postmillennialism*.) Another position, amillennialism, is the position most commonly seen in Churches of Christ today. Amillennialists (literally, no-millennialists) believe that purported biblical references to the millennium are allegorical or nonliteral in nature; as a result, they do not believe that there will be an actual period of one thousand years of divine rule preceding or following the Second Coming.

The interpretation which caused so much controversy in Churches of Christ in the early twentieth century, however, was a form of premillennialism known as dispensationalism. Broadly speaking, premillennialism is the belief that only the direct return of Jesus to the Earth will be enough to bring about the millennium—human effort alone will not and cannot suffice. (Predictably, the viewpoint is known as *premillennialism* because Christ's return has to *precede* the *millennium.*) Dispensational premillennialism adds a few details to this system. Dispensationalists divide human history into seven periods, or "dispensations." We live in the current "Church Age," under this schema, because Jewish resistance to Jesus prevented the full establishment of God's kingdom. The end of the Church Age, within the dispensationalist view, will be foreshadowed by a period of suffering, or tribulation, for believers—the Antichrist and false prophet will seize power, Armageddon will occur, and there will perhaps be a rapture of the faithful.

Dispensational premillennialism grew rapidly in popularity in the wider Christian world at the turn of the twentieth century, and the main proponent of the position within Churches of Christ was R.H. Boll. In 1910, Boll joined the editorial staff of the *Gospel Advocate*, and within a few years, he had started publishing articles outlining his beliefs about the millennium. Some of Boll's coworkers and fellow *Advocate* contributors were troubled by this, and Boll eventually resigned in 1915. Yet even as Boll's teachings gained some ground during the 1920s, members of Churches of Christ generally felt that this kind of speculation about the end times was not worth dividing over.

This precarious balance was upset during the 1930s. Many writers and preachers became increasingly severe in their public criticism of premillennialism, perhaps none more so than Foy E. Wallace, Jr.—quite possibly the single most influential person in Churches of Christ during the first half of the twentieth century. Wallace's writings and speeches often lambasted those who held premillennialist views, as well as those who simply believed that the doctrine was not worth dividing over. Wallace's critique of premillennialist theology stemmed from his strongly held belief that the system was an addition to, rather than an interpretation of, the New Testament.

Fierce criticism notwithstanding, R.H. Boll continued to carry the banner of premillennialism within Churches of Christ, and he never wavered from his convictions, even as numerous former allies publicly denounced his teachings and he found himself increasingly isolated within the fellowship. Yet by the 1940s, perhaps even earlier, his struggle was a losing battle. Boll ultimately passed away in 1956, and while some Churches of Christ (mostly in Louisiana and Kentucky, where Boll worked for many years) still hold premillennialist views today, they are a distinct minority.

What are the lasting legacies of the controversy over premillennialism? For one, the division did much to define the eschatology of a majority of Churches of Christ. Whereas Churches of Christ—and the broader nineteenth-century movement that they had been part of—had been home to a variety of views on the millennium, from this point forward, the amillennial view would hold sway. In fact, the position became so dominant that it was not always even referred to by name but was often simply presented as the single proper system of belief about the end times.

The premillennial controversy also proved to be significant for Churches of Christ because it established a pattern (of sorts) for how future theological conflicts would be resolved. The sharp criticisms and shrewd maneuverings of Wallace and other opponents of premillennialism to isolate their foes were, if nothing else, effective; in the end, out of all of the colleges and newspapers affiliated with Churches of Christ, only Boll's *Word and Work* paper defended premillennialism. Wallace, to be sure, also alienated many who doctrinally agreed with him. R.H. Boll was generally well-liked, and even some of those who had no love for Boll's teachings felt that Wallace's heated rhetoric was inappropriate.

Regardless, a very similar series of events would play out over the following decades, when Churches of Christ would once again be confronted with the possibility of division. Whereas premillennialism had been the spark that ignited controversy during the 1930s, debates in the middle of the twentieth century would center on church-sponsored institutions like colleges, orphanages, and missions programs.

Discussion Questions

1. Were you aware of the early twentieth century controversy over premillennialism within Churches of Christ? If so, what did you know about the division before this chapter?

2. What are your views on the existence (or not) of a literal millennium? Do you know other members of Churches of Christ who believe differently from you?

3. How should large, fellowship-wide divisions such as the premillennialism debate be handled? Is division the appropriate, even necessary, response? Or is there room for some divergence of opinion on certain matters?

— 8 —

THE INSTITUTIONALISM DEBATE

Last chapter, we explored the early twentieth century controversy over dispensational premillennialism within Churches of Christ. Although there previously had been a variety of teachings and beliefs about the end times within the movement—Alexander Campbell and many other antebellum restorationists had held post-millennial views, for instance—going forward, amillennialism would become the most common position within our fellowship. (The amillennial viewpoint, of course, holds that possible biblical references to a millennium are figurative or symbolic in nature.) In addition to this eschatological legacy, we saw a "playbook" established, for better or for worse, which many leaders in Churches of Christ would rely on during future periods of division—a pattern of publicly criticizing and separating from one's opponents en masse. This pattern proved to have great significance for the debate over institutionalism within Churches of Christ during the middle of the twentieth century.

The post-World War Two period was a time of explosive growth throughout the American religious world, and Churches of Christ were part of this postwar boom. A vast array of junior colleges associated with the movement sprang up during the 1940s and 1950s, including Alabama Christian College (now Faulkner University) and Florida Christian College (now Florida College). Several of the colleges which already existed, such as Harding and Pepperdine, engaged in significant expansions as well. Much of this nationwide boom in higher education stemmed from the GI Bill, which made it possible for many veterans who might not have otherwise gone to college to do so.

Nor were the growing colleges the only institutions that brought Churches of Christ prestige on the national stage. In the early 1950s, under the oversight of the Highland Church of Christ in Abilene, Texas, many congregations banded together to undertake a massive radio and television evangelism program known as the "Herald of Truth." Because of the size and scope of the project, Highland began seeking financial assistance from Churches of Christ across the nation. (This "sponsoring church" approach, you might have already guessed, would come to feature prominently in debates over institutionalization in the years to come.) Taken collectively, the numerical growth of Churches of Christ in the postwar era—along with the accompanying growth of the movement's colleges, mission efforts, lectureships, and media outreach—indicated that the fellowship was on the rise, increasingly comfortable as a major religious group in the United States and, to a somewhat lesser extent, abroad.

Yet many of these developments would have been unwelcome or even unimaginable to many in earlier generations of Churches of Christ, and a sizable portion of the fellowship registered its concerns about such changes around the middle of the twentieth century. Initially, the colleges associated with the movement were the focal point of the growing debate over institutions, partly because of their size and partly because of their potential influence on future generations of leaders and members within Churches of Christ. Although there were debates over the proper relationship between the schools and local churches, as well as over the propriety of the schools offering athletic and other extracurricular activities, the most important question ultimately proved to be how the colleges were funded. Throughout the 1930s, most schools accepted contributions from congregations occasionally, though some were skeptical of the practice, seeing it as an improper use of church funds and a threat to the authority of the elders and local congregations.

The Second World War brought with it a temporary halt to the discussion about schools and other such institutions, but as Churches of Christ and their programs expanded in the postwar period, the issue came roaring back to the forefront. 1949 proved to be a consequential year for the debate over institutionalism because of the initial publication of the *Gospel Guardian*, an avowedly anti-institutional newspaper. Leading figures Roy Cogdill, Fanning Yater Tant, and Cled Wallace spoke out against arrangements like the "sponsoring church" system, in which smaller congregations could contribute financially to a project or mission effort overseen by a larger church. This arrangement did avoid the creation of a separate missionary society, yet critics like Cogdill, Tant, and Wallace were not convinced that there was any scriptural precedent for it, either.

Aside from the theological issues underpinning the debate, the disagreement over the growing institutionalism of Churches of Christ could also turn incredibly personal, often to the point of absurdity. Foy E. Wallace Jr., as was often the case during the premillennial controversy, was quick to attack his opponents' character. In response to his name-calling, one member of a rival paper's editorial board wrote him a letter asking if he would like to be called "Foy-somebody-else-pays-his-bills-Wallace," a not-so-subtle dig at Wallace's frequent financial troubles. Too, N.B. Hardeman called *Gospel*

Guardian editor Fanning Yater Tant "a degenerate son of a noble sire," implying that while Tant's father J.D. had been worthy of praise, the apple had fallen a considerable distance from the tree.[14]

More notable still was the effort of *Gospel Advocate* editor B.C. Goodpasture to publicize an intra-congregational dispute in Lufkin, Texas. Roy Cogdill and Cled Wallace, both on the *Gospel Guardian* staff, wound up on opposite sides of a church split and came to serve as the preachers of the two congregations which emerged from the division. Even though the split had nothing to do with institutional issues, Goodpasture pointed to the incident as evidence that the non-institutional wing of Churches of Christ was inherently divisive, even to the point of rending its own congregations in two.

After several years of back-and-forth between the two sides, Goodpasture publicly called for a fellowship-wide "quarantine" of his opponents. In late 1954, he

14. Letter from C.B.F. Young to Foy E. Wallace, Jr., January 27, 1941. Quoted in David Edwin Harrell Jr., *The Churches of Christ in the Twentieth Century: Homer Hailey's Personal Journey of Faith* (Tuscaloosa, AL: The University of Alabama Press, 2000), 107; Letter from N.B. Hardeman to B.C. Goodpasture, December 21, 1957. Quoted in John C. Hardin, "Rock Fights, Quarantines, and Confessionals: B.C. Goodpasture, the *Gospel Advocate*, and Keeping Order in Churches of Christ," in *Recovering the Margins of American Religious History: The Legacy of David Edwin Harrell Jr.*, eds. B. Dwain Waldrep and Scott Billingsley (Tuscaloosa, AL: The University of Alabama Press, 2012), 73.

published a letter and series of comments in the *Advocate* which called for a system to identify noninstitutional preachers, ostensibly for the purpose of helping congregations avoid hiring divisive preachers for pulpit ministerial positions. Goodpasture's endorsement of the plan led to a great deal of consternation on the part of the *Guardian*'s staff and readership, but many on Goodpasture's side were supportive of the step. Their attacks on the non-institutional position had already forced some preachers to publicly declare for the pro-institutional side, and in 1957, Goodpasture began printing "confessionals" written by former non-institutionalists who, for whatever reason, had recanted that position—Foy Wallace, most notably, but also figures like the prominent Alabama preacher John D. Cox.

By the end of the 1950s and into the early 1960s, the division between the two factions was almost complete. The noninstitutional congregations, which comprised about ten percent of Churches of Christ, would henceforth turn their attention to building up their own congregations, newspapers, and school (Florida College) in the years to come, while many in the institutional churches gradually forgot what the division had initially been over. (The debate was not just about kitchens, as is often misremembered today!)

While the mid-century debate over institutions can best be understood as an attempt by more conservative members to influence "mainstream" or more middle-of-the-road congregations, theologically progressive members of Churches of Christ would also try to shift the conversation within the movement in the decades to come. Indeed, as we will see over the next few chapters, Churches of Christ would be pulled in a variety of directions, and advocates of unity would have a difficult task on their hands.

Discussion Questions

1. How did outside events, such as the passage of the GI Bill and subsequent rise in college enrollments after World War Two, impact decisions made within Churches of Christ?

2. What do you think was the root issue of the institutional division? Did the two sides interpret scripture differently, or did they simply differ as to whether certain practices threatened the authority of individual congregations?

3. What role do institutions, such as colleges and newspapers—or websites and lectureships—play in shaping the life of the church today?

9

Drifting Apart
Part One

Over the last two chapters, we have seen two significant theological issues—the proper understanding of biblical teachings on the millennium, and the scriptural authority for church-related institutions—lead to formal divisions within Churches of Christ. Over the coming chapters, however, we will see that theological conflict often led to a gradual drifting apart rather than a single heated conflict and official separation. This chapter, we'll bring our story up through the late 1970s, exploring the various directions different members of Churches of Christ sought to take the movement, even as they all continued to share the larger common goal of restoring first century Christianity.

Broadly speaking, Americans were not quite as churchgoing in the 1960s as they had been during the 1950s, yet somewhere in the neighborhood of forty percent continued to attend church services regularly. Many of these believers were troubled by various political and social developments during the 1960s, and members of Churches of Christ, like all people, were impacted by events outside of their control. One major change they had to respond to was the election of the country's first Catholic president, John F. Kennedy, in 1960. Like many Protestant Christians, many members of Churches of Christ feared that the president would, in effect, be a mere puppet of the pope. This increased concern for electoral politics reveals a significant shift away from the apoliticism of David Lipscomb and others in previous generations of the fellowship.

Alongside Catholicism, communism was a grave concern for members of Churches of Christ, as it was for most Americans. The Vietnam War provides an excellent case study. To be sure, editors of publications associated with Churches of Christ rarely defended the war per se, but they were often critical of those who protested the war, portraying them as Marxists who sought to overthrow the federal government. The *Gospel Advocate*, on occasion, even published materials from FBI director J. Edgar Hoover warning about communist takeovers of college campuses. Again, this kind of political engagement more closely resembled the worldview of the restorationists who, decades earlier, had backed the candidacy of James A. Garfield—restorationists who were more likely to end up in the Disciples of Christ than in Churches of Christ.

While members of Churches of Christ were, by and large, politically conservative, they were less in agreement on a number of religious matters. Dating back to the late 1950s, a small group within the fellowship, including men like Leroy Garrett and Carl Ketcherside, sought to reintroduce a greater desire for Christian unity into a group which, as we have seen, was often divided against itself. Garrett and Ketcherside spoke out against what they saw as a very exclusive, denominational attitude within Churches of Christ. Although the two men and those sympathetic to their views were often shunned or marginalized within the larger body of Churches of Christ, they, like other individuals scattered throughout the history of the movement, offered a more gracious perspective and challenged the exclusivist and confrontational mindset which has, at times, been the default within our fellowship.

Too, members of Churches of Christ who held advanced degrees and were conversant with the wider world of biblical scholarship sought to connect others within in the fellowship to those kinds of resources and conversations. For instance, Abraham Malherbe and Pat Harrell started an academic journal called *Restoration Quarterly*, giving it the twofold task of (1) allowing scholars within Churches of Christ to share their research and (2) presenting to readers developments taking place in the broader world of biblical scholarship. While *ResQ* was primarily targeted at academics, popular periodicals like *Integrity* and *Mission* sought to redirect the general reader's focus away from the overriding issues and concerns of previous generations and toward the social and ethical issues of the day. It was also during this period that several of the colleges affiliated with Churches of Christ sought out greater academic respectability, adding graduate-level theological programs and bolstering their faculties with the alumni of prestigious universities and seminaries.

These kinds of developments were not universally applauded, however, and others within Churches of Christ expressed concern about what they described as "liberalism" and "modernism" entering their fellowship. These conservatives, including Freed-Hardeman professor Thomas B. Warren and missionary Ira Y. Rice, Jr., created new journals like the *Spiritual Sword* and *Contending for the Faith* to defend their understanding of the restoration vision. Those in this more conservative wing also established new preacher training schools during this era, partly because of a movement-wide shortage of ministers and partly because of increased concern about the training provided at the universities. These journals and schools, Ed Harrell notes, formed the backbone of an "alternate institutional network" to rival   the   older   publications   and   universities.[15]

One other major turning point from this period bears mentioning —the development of campus ministry efforts within Churches of Christ. Like many Christian fellowships in the U.S. South and elsewhere, Churches of Christ focused much of their collective attention on college campuses in the post-World War Two era, when enrollments swelled to record levels and aging congregations began to seek infusions of younger members. These efforts built on previous generations' attempts to bridge the gap between church and campus. In fact, interest in outreach at schools not directly affiliated with Churches of Christ dates back at least to the 1910s, when Jesse P. Sewell, an educational advocate within Churches of Christ and the president of Abilene Christian College, sought to create an explicitly Christian dormitory at the University of Texas and to offer an option for students living there to take Bible classes for college credit. By the 1950s, Churches of Christ had managed to establish "Bible chairs" at Texas and several other schools, which taught college-level Bible classes to interested students. This movement even spawned its own religious periodical, the *Bible Chair Journal.*

15. Harrell, *The Churches of Christ in the Twentieth Century,* 189.

The "Bible chair" movement was not primarily an evangelistic program, however, since most of its efforts were focused on training students already affiliated with Churches of Christ who happened to attend public schools. In the 1960s, a younger generation of leaders within the fellowship began pointing out the need for a more direct emphasis on evangelism. Key in this regard was Wesley Reagan, who in 1965 called for Churches of Christ to unite their individual campus ministries under one national organization, which was known as Campus Evangelism during its brief existence.

Under the oversight of leaders like Jim Bevis, Rex Vermillion, and John Allen Chalk, Campus Evangelism made remarkable progress in bringing together Churches of Christ campus ministry leaders and thinkers during the 1960s. Its seminars trained thousands of students and sought to refocus the fellowship's attention on the person of Jesus, rather than on doctrinal disputes over the use of instrumental music in worship and similar issues. Campus Evangelism also pushed beyond the white, conservative, suburban, middle class boundaries of Churches of Christ, prioritizing outreach to students of color and from all across the political spectrum. Yet the backlash to some of Campus Evangelism's other activities was fierce, and by 1970, the group had basically ceased to exist. In the following chapter, we'll outline that story and explore some of the long-term impacts of campus ministry efforts within Churches of Christ, including the development of the discipling/Boston Movement churches.

Discussion Questions

1. What issues drove members of Churches of Christ to engage more directly with politics during the 1950s and 1960s? How did this increased involvement resemble or differ from the actions of those in earlier generations?

2. What role did the competing sets of institutions (colleges and preaching schools, newspapers, and lectureships) play in the gradual drifting apart of Churches of Christ during the 1960s and 1970s?

3. What role have campus ministries of one form or another played in your life? Had you heard of the "Bible chair" programs before?

— 10 —

GAINESVILLE, BOSTON, AND LOS ANGELES

At the close of our last chapter, we began tracing the history of campus ministry efforts within Churches of Christ, starting with the "Bible chair" movement and ending with the creation of an impressive but controversial organization known as Campus Evangelism. This time, we'll continue to follow that campus ministry thread as we build up to two of the most significant developments in our fellowship's recent history: the creation of the discipling movement within Churches of Christ and the splitting off of a separate religious fellowship known as the International Churches of Christ.

As we noted before, Campus Evangelism provoked a significant backlash despite its apparent effectiveness in evangelistic outreach. The organization's structure had been heavily influenced by similar campus ministry efforts taking place in other Christian traditions, and to many within Churches of Christ, it seemed to threaten the congregational autonomy so prized by the movement. Other skeptics raised concerns about the group's emphasis on the activity of the Holy Spirit. These and other objections were voiced at an "Open Forum" held in 1969 at Freed-Hardeman College (now Freed-Hardeman University) in Henderson, Tennessee. The criticisms raised at this event negatively impacted the reputation of Campus Evangelism, along with its ability to fundraise, and the organization faded away soon after.

Although Campus Evangelism was short-lived, its influence continued to be felt throughout Churches of Christ during the following decades. One of the most remarkable (and most successful) efforts inspired by the group was located at the Crossroads Church of Christ in Gainesville, Florida, home of the University of Florida. This program, led by Chuck Lucas, established a new paradigm for campus ministry in the movement. Lucas combined Campus Evangelism's focus on college outreach with a set of "discipling" techniques developed by charismatic Christian groups to form a one-on-one mentoring system which encouraged all members to share their faith regularly and held them accountable if they did not. Though controversial in its own right, this approach led to unprecedented rates of growth at Crossroads. In fact, Lucas came to be seen as something of a campus ministry guru during the 1960s and 1970s, and Churches of Christ across the United States began sending their ministers to Crossroads to be "discipled" by Lucas, after which training, they would return home and establish similar campus ministries at their churches.

It was, however, Lucas's discipling program that caused tension between Crossroads-influenced congregations and other Churches of Christ. Objections over a lack of scriptural backing for many of Lucas's practices were raised, but a more impactful line of attack was that the strict controls and extreme accountability of the discipling program had effectively turned the discipling movement into a cult. College ministers from other Christian traditions protested the group's presence on different campuses as well. Eventually, partly because of the controversy and partly because of personal issues, Lucas was asked to resign from his ministry position at the Crossroads church in 1985. Yet even by that time, the Crossroads movement had already begun to transform, and the center of authority within that sphere had shifted from Gainesville, Florida, to Boston, Massachusetts, where a Lucas disciple named Kip McKean was making waves within Churches of Christ and beyond.

Kip McKean became the minister of the Lexington congregation (located in the Boston metro area) in 1979, and under his leadership, the church swelled in number—growing from fifty members to over three

thousand and moving its services from a tiny building
to the Boston Garden arena. The congregation, which
became known as the Boston Church of Christ, planted
or "reconstructed" likeminded congregations in large
cities, both domestically and abroad, with the attend-
ance of many of these congregations reaching into the
thousands. But, like the churches which had followed
Lucas's lead a decade earlier, the congregations influenced by McKean faced accusations of cult-like
practices and teachings, and students on several campuses across the nation reported harassment and threats
from church members. Some of McKean's harshest critics were members of Churches of Christ who did not
adopt the discipling methodology and who were skeptical of the power he had accumulated at the top of this
"Boston Movement."

Throughout the 1980s, the churches in the Boston
orbit began to separate themselves from the larger body
of Churches of Christ—and vice versa. Several factors,
both theological and otherwise, led to this division. For
one, McKean had adapted the common restoration re-
frain of "speaking where the Bible speaks and remaining
silent where it is silent" into "remaining silent where the
Bible speaks and speaking where it is silent." This seemingly minor adjustment reflected a major shift regarding
scriptural silence and whether such silence is permissive
or restrictive. Too, the groups diverged in matters of

church polity and governance. Whereas Churches of Christ have historically prided themselves on their devotion to congregational autonomy, the churches within the Boston Movement submitted willingly to a larger system of ecclesiastical oversight, with McKean himself at the top. Other causes could be mentioned, including heated personal disputes involving parties on both sides. Suffice it to say that as the 1980s rolled into the 1990s, this movement-within-a-movement, which had originally sought to revitalize Churches of Christ, had all but broken away from the larger fellowship.

During the 1990s, seeking a more prominent location for the flagship church of the movement, McKean relocated from Boston to the Los Angeles Church of Christ. Around the same time, his movement took on the new name of "International Churches of Christ," a name that reflected its worldwide aspirations and historical connections to Churches of Christ. The ICOC, like the Boston and Crossroads movements before it, grew rapidly throughout the decade. McKean challenged his fellow believers to establish an ICOC congregation in every nation with a city of at least 100,000 people by the year 2000, and by the turn of the millennium, there were over 400 congregations and nearly 200,000 regular Sunday attendees within the movement.

Yet even though the ICOC's public image grew stronger throughout the 1990s, the underlying reality was somewhat less rosy. Church plantings continued to rise, but actual membership numbers did not. The church's extreme demands for financial giving, as well as the constant shuffling of leaders between congregations and even countries, led to an incredibly high turnover rate for new members. Ultimately, after years of concerns about abuses of the discipling methodology and about McKean's tight control of the movement, McKean was effectively forced to resign in late 2001. This kicked off a period of soul-searching for the ICOC. A number of other leaders, including those of the Boston church, publicly apologized for errors made during their tenure. Also notable was a widely shared 2003 open letter by London evangelist Henry Kriete, which was highly critical of McKean's leadership over the previous decade.

This period of internal turmoil for the ICOC did lead to some renewal of the ties between that fellowship and the larger body of Churches of Christ. In 2004, a handful of ICOC leaders attended the Abilene Christian University lectureship, where they spoke both privately and publicly about the previous decades and sought some measure of fellowship, or at least rapprochement, with their counterparts in Churches of Christ. Meaningful efforts were made to reduce the size of the ICOC's worldwide hierarchy and to modify its discipling practices. These changes did not sit well with McKean and those loyal to him, however, and in 2006, he led a splinter group (known as the International Christian Church or Sold-Out Discipling Movement) to break away from the ICOC. Only time will tell what the long-term ramifications of these developments will be, both for Churches of Christ and for the ICOC.

Discussion Questions

1. Were you aware of the developments surrounding the discipling and Boston movements during the 1970s and 1980s? Was your congregation impacted in any way by either of those movements, or by the ICOC during the 1990s?

2. How significant was Kip McKean's revision of the restoration aim of "speaking where the Bible speaks"? What impact might such a change have on the way the Bible is read?

3. Did you know that McKean was no longer affiliated with the International Churches of Christ, or that he had created a new fellowship of churches during the 2000s?

— 11 —

DRIFTING APART
PART TWO

Since we spent most of our space in the last chapter tracing the history of the International Churches of Christ, we would be remiss to not also cover developments within Churches of Christ during that same era. We'll do just that in this last regular chapter of the book. (The following two chapters are devoted to thematic studies rather than to the general narrative.)

Perhaps the single most important story in the history of Churches of Christ in recent decades has been the growing debate over hermeneutics, or ways of reading Scripture. Traditionally, Churches of Christ have approached the New Testament as a source of truths contained in three forms: direct commands to do something (or not), binding examples of the early church doing something (or not), and necessary inferences from the texts which guide believers to do something (or not). Using these three categories, New Testament "law" could be established and clear teachings on the issues be discerned. But by the 1980s and 1990s, this approach to reading Scripture was no longer a given. Many figures within Churches of Christ began to assert that this way of looking at the Bible overly prioritized human actions and neglected to adequately present the overriding message of God's grace towards us which, they argued, was the central theme of Scripture. Though many individual Churches of Christ never openly reckoned with this hermeneutical debate, the broader discussion within our fellowship revealed the variety of theological assumptions that all parties, from the most hermeneutically conservative to the most progressive, brought to the biblical texts.

Disagreements over the "new hermeneutic" and other practices and teachings undoubtedly were influenced by members' beliefs about what the Bible taught, but as always, there was also a sociological component to such disputes. Churches of Christ, once a fellowship of believers who frequently worshipped in small, inexpensive buildings in rural areas, had—as a whole— become significantly better educated and better off financially over the latter half of the twentieth century. Yet these and related developments were not uniformly spread throughout the movement. One survey from the early 1990s revealed that approximately twenty percent of Churches of Christ had more than one paid minister on staff, that roughly two-thirds of these ministers had a bachelor's degree, and that about a third held some sort of graduate degree to boot. There was also a notable correlation between the amount of education the minister had and the size of the congregation they worked for, however, with more educated ministers being more likely to serve larger congregations.

Another important sociological development has been the continued growth of multiple competing sets of institutions, such as colleges, lectureships, and news outlets, which are more closely affiliated with either conservative or progressive Churches of Christ. Publications like the *Gospel Advocate* and lectureships like Freed-Hardeman University's, for instance, fall into the former category, while *Wineskins* and the Pepperdine lectures exemplify the latter. The seeming self-separation of believers into one of these two camps has not yet lead to a formal schism within Churches of Christ, though the growing division has certainly impacted our fellowship. One additional factor which has been both a cause and an effect of this separation has been the decline of many of the periodicals, television shows, and radio programs which had reached Churches of Christ nationwide in earlier generations.

One last example of just how divergent the paths taken by Churches of Christ had become can be found in the ministry of Max Lucado, a famous preacher and author located in San Antonio, Texas. During the 1990s, Lucado was almost certainly the most well-known figure within Churches of Christ, with several best-selling books that reached large audiences in both Churches of Christ and the broader Christian reading world. Lucado was also a leading voice of a growing unity movement located within some of the more theologically progressive Churches of Christ, a movement which sought to move away from the exclusivist perspective of previous generations and to acknowledge and emphasize the common ground shared by Churches of Christ and other Christian groups. This mindset was applauded by many but strongly criticized by others who believed that the Bible provided clear limits on how far Christian fellowship could extend.

On a somewhat lighter note, one other notable change within the last few decades has been the increasing fame achieved by individual members of Churches of Christ in a variety of fields and endeavors. Certainly, there had been well-known figures within Churches of Christ and the united movement of the nineteenth century—James A. Garfield, for instance, was elected to the presidency in 1880—but celebrities have become more prevalent within the movement all the same. Entertainers as widely divergent as "Weird Al" Yankovic and the Robertson family of *Duck Dynasty* fame claim membership in Churches of Christ, as have leading social and political figures like civil rights attorney Fred Gray, news anchor Lester Holt, and U.S. Senator John Cornyn of Texas. The prominence of these members has brought no small amount of attention to Churches of Christ—sometimes positive, sometimes less so—but reflects the increased cultural salience of individuals within our fellowship all the same.

That brings our story to a close for this chapter. Over the following two chapters, we will take a slightly different tack, turning our attention to two stories-within-the-story of Churches of Christ that we have not covered in any meaningful depth so far: the history of predominantly black Churches of Christ (chapter twelve), and the history of women within Churches of Christ (chapter thirteen). To this point, our focus has, of course, largely focused on white men within Churches of Christ. This is because the lion's share of the most visible roles within our fellowship—ministers, elders, and deacons, but also authors, editors, organizers, and similar positions—have been held by white men. But to neglect the stories we will highlight over the next two chapters would be a disservice to the richness of our movement's history and to the legacies of those Christians whose life stories often played out far from the spotlight but who made major contributions to the Kingdom all the same.

Discussion Questions

1. What church-affiliated institutions does your congregation have the closest ties to? Does your congregation retain connections to Churches of Christ who might hold different views on the hermeneutical debate or related issues? Why or why not?

2. What about you? Do you have family members, friends, coworkers, or other acquaintances who are members of Churches of Christ that might differ in some way from your own? Again, why or why not?

3. Were you aware that the celebrities listed above have ties to Churches of Christ? Have you heard or read about other famous figures with connections to our fellowship? What are the potential benefits and pitfalls of having prominent members such as these?

— 12 —

THE BLACK CHURCH EXPERIENCE

As we mentioned at the end of the previous chapter, the final two chapters in this book on the history of Churches of Christ will follow a slightly different format from the previous eleven, tracing a smaller story-within-a-story over a longer period of time to provide a more complete picture of our shared history than we have seen so far.

This time, our study focuses on the history of predominantly black Churches of Christ. This narrative, in some instances, overlaps with the stories we've covered so far, but in other cases, it diverges from them—often because of the prejudices held by many white Christians who kept black believers at arm's length or further away.

At the end of the American Civil War and the abolition of slavery, the largest concentrations of black members of the restoration churches were in former slave states like Kentucky and Virginia. Most of these approximately 7,000 men and women were members in

majority-white congregations, but over time, many separate majority-black congregations would be formed
instead. White members of Churches of Christ often as-
sisted with these projects, financially or otherwise, yet
their motives were often less than charitable. (Their desire to conform to the Jim Crow segregation of the day
was at least as strong of a motivating factor as the goal
of reaching black Americans with the gospel.) In any
case, these efforts were successful from a numerical
standpoint, with more than 50,000 black Christians
added by the turn of the twentieth century. Such growth
largely resulted from the tireless efforts of the itinerant
(traveling) black preachers who held a steady string of
gospel meetings and established congregations wher-
ever they went. Another important contribution of this
generation was the creation of schools for black students, even though these institutions faced difficult
financial situations (at best) and apathy or outright hos-
tility from white Christians (at worst).

Relatively few black members of restoration churches
had the power to speak out against the evils of Jim Crow
segregation directly, though there were certainly exceptions. One such critic was Preston Taylor, a prominent
black businessman who worked to protest the adoption
of segregation laws in his hometown of Nashville, Tennessee. Other men and women resisted or simply hoped
to survive segregation in different ways—for instance,

by establishing schools or, in the case of the black restorers who would later affiliate with the Disciples of Christ, creating their own associations and assemblies within that fellowship.

One notable leader within predominantly black Churches of Christ in the early twentieth century was George Philip (G.P.) Bowser, who had grown up in the Methodist Church and who had been trained at a Methodist college. Bowser, among his many evangelistic pursuits, established several schools throughout his lifetime, and many future black leaders within Churches of Christ were trained at Bowser's schools. In 1902, Bowser also founded the *Christian Echo*, which has undoubtedly been the single most influential periodical among black members of Churches of Christ ever since. Bowser student Richard Nathaniel (R.N.) Hogan would later edit the *Echo* himself, and he used the publication to (rightly) call out white Christians for their complicity in, or even support of, racial segregation.

Another crucial figure within the history of black Churches of Christ during the twentieth century—perhaps the single most well-known figure—was Marshall Keeble, a preacher who converted thousands at the massive gospel meetings and revivals he held throughout his career. Keeble rarely directly addressed racial issues in his preaching, as his ministry was largely dependent on financial support from white segregationists within

Churches of Christ, many of whom lauded Keeble for his seemingly single-minded devotion to preaching the gospel. Yet Keeble's ability to draw financial support from Christians who often saw him as their racial inferior and his use of those funds to share the gospel to black (and white) audiences—to say nothing of his training of another generation of leaders, such as noted civil rights attorney Fred Gray, who would be less hesitant to speak out against the racial status quo—revealed that Keeble, in his own way, sought to challenge the racist worldviews held by many of his fellow Christians.

For all of their differences in style, the lives of Bowser and Keeble help illustrate the larger history of predominantly black Churches of Christ. These congregations, like their counterparts in most, if not all, American Christian traditions, frequently faced prejudice from white Christians who might have seen them as equals before God, but not in any other setting. Because white members of Churches of Christ tended to understand sin as solely an individual matter, rather than as a collective one, they often overlooked societal evils and injustices and were slow to speak out against racism within their own fellowship. This prejudice effectively led to the creation of a movement-within-the-movement as majority-black congregations were established across the nation—not because black Christians necessarily chose to separate from their white brothers and sisters, but because they were excluded from the racially segregated congregations which already existed. According to one estimate, predominantly black Churches of Christ totaled more than 1,200 congregations as of 1990. Black Christians continue to sponsor lectureships, periodicals, and even Southwestern Christian College, institutions which remain fixtures in church life today.

Speaking of higher education, the other colleges and universities associated with Churches of Christ showed varying degrees of responsiveness to Supreme Court decisions, such as *Brown v. Board of Education* (1954), which integrated the nation's schools. In practice, many remained almost completely segregated for some time, though nominal (and in certain cases more substantive) integration had taken place by the early 1970s. Experiences could differ somewhat from school to school. Pepperdine, for instance, admitted black students from the time of its founding in 1937, yet those students were not originally allowed to live in on-campus housing. Southeastern Institute of the Bible (now Heritage Christian University), which was founded in 1968, did not enroll its first African American student until 1972, but there was never a policy of segregation or racial exclusion at the institution. Other exceptions to the general pattern may exist. In any event, beginning in the 1990s, leaders of several of the movement's schools began to publicly acknowledge the past wrongs committed by their institutions, to ask for forgiveness from black brothers and sisters in Christ, and to set the stage for ongoing and future efforts towards reconciliation.

Discussion Questions

1. In what ways have members of Churches of Christ been influenced by the racial attitudes (at times, the prejudices) of the larger cultural contexts they have inhabited? Why must the church always be on guard against these kinds of negative cultural influences?

2. Do the congregations of Churches of Christ in your general area seem to reflect the pattern of division and segregation outlined in this chapter? If so, why might that be?

3. What role do individual believers have in fostering better relationships across racial and other divisions within Churches of Christ?

— 13 —

THE HISTORY OF WOMEN WITHIN CHURCHES OF CHRIST

We have covered much ground together over the last twelve chapters. We have talked about the nineteenth-century currents which gave rise to a generation of Christians who sought the restoration of the first-century faith in their own time. We have seen both the tremendous successes and frequent setbacks they and likeminded believers in subsequent generations encountered. Too, we have also zoomed in to focus on a story-within-a-story: the history of predominantly black Churches of Christ. In this chapter, we conclude our study with one more topic that has its own special focus: the history of women within Churches of Christ. We'll begin by going back to the nineteenth century to talk about women's various roles in the churches of this larger restoration movement before narrowing our focus to Churches of Christ during the twentieth century and beyond.

Although few women held any sort of official role within restoration churches during the early-to-middle nineteenth century, examples of women who nevertheless spoke and acted with courage and conviction can still be seen in the historical record. For instance, as you may remember, we learned about the Christadelphian movement a few chapters back. In part, John Thomas and his followers had broken with Alexander Campbell and many of the other restorers over the practice of re-baptizing converts from other Christian traditions. (Thomas, we should remember, was in favor of it, though at the time, his was the minority opinion.) In 1837, Campbell received an anonymous letter which strongly criticized his teachings on the issue; he printed large portions of the letter and responded to them in the pages of his newspaper. Only within the last decade or so has the author of this letter been identified, however. The willingness and ability of Louisa Anderson, an early convert of Thomas's, to challenge a powerful figure like Campbell should remind us that women of her era were not blindly and uniformly submissive to men on church matters, especially those in which they had a vested interest.

There were also a very small number of female evangelists within nineteenth-century restoration circles, though most were traveling, or itinerant, preachers and were not located at (or supported by) a particular congregation. The earliest of these restorationist itinerant women was Nancy Gove Cram, who was affiliated with the "Christians only" or "Christian Connexion" movement. Cram was born in 1776, and for at least a few years during the 1810s, she travelled around upstate New York establishing congregations and holding revival meetings. Perhaps the first woman to actually be ordained in a Stone-Campbell Movement fellowship was Melissa Garrett Terrell, who was ordained by the Ebenezer Christian Church in Ohio in 1867, though several other women were likewise ordained around the same time.

Another notable figure, one who you may have already heard of in a history class at school, is the famous temperance (anti-alcohol) activist Carrie Nation. Nation, who studied at a movement-affiliated school and who was baptized at a Missouri gospel meeting, hosted a congregation in her Texas home during the 1880s. (In an unusual connection, Nation's mother was also a distant relative of Alexander Campbell.) Her claim to have received the baptism of the Holy Spirit and her insistence that women had the authority to preach led to her being disfellowshipped in the 1890s, though she remained a sought-after speaker and preacher for the Women's Christian Temperance Union for many years to come.

Women like Cram and Nation were the exceptions who proved the rule regarding women's involvement in preaching in the restoration churches during the nineteenth century. They almost universally justified their actions by expressing the belief that no person had the right to prevent them from using their God-given talents—though a majority of their fellow believers seemed to disagree, as evidenced by the difficult and often lonely paths these women travelled. Some nineteenth-century Churches of Christ seem to have allowed women to serve as deacons (or deaconesses), particularly congregations which were more closely associated with Barton W. Stone than with Alexander Campbell. By the turn of the twentieth century, however, most had reduced or eliminated the practice.

In fact, the proper roles of women in the local congregation had become a hot-button issue within restoration circles by the 1880s, as some of the more progressive churches had begun opening up opportunities for women to serve with the Christian Woman's Board of Missions during the previous decade. This move was often characterized by more conservative restorers as yet another "digression" on the part of the progressives, much like the use of instrumental music in worship or the creation of the American Christian Missionary Society. The 1906 recognition of the schism between the Disciples of Christ and Churches of Christ also had the effect of crystallizing the division between those who approved (at least at some level) of women serving in formal leadership roles and those who did not.

Yet the debate was not conclusively settled at this juncture. Silena Holman, the wife of an elder of a Church of Christ in Tennessee, challenged the fellowship's traditional beliefs about the proper roles of women in the congregation and in the home. Her frequent letters to David Lipscomb's *Gospel Advocate* paper reveal her belief that there was no fundamental difference between a woman speaking about religious matters to a mixed-gender audience at home and her doing so in a congregational setting. While Holman's perspective was undoubtedly a minority view, her example does show us that there was not complete uniformity of belief on this matter, even at this point. (Also worth noting is that Holman, like Carry Nation, was a leading figure within the temperance movement; she became the president of a Tennessee statewide temperance organization in 1896.)

Holman and a few likeminded believers notwithstanding, there was a general consensus within Churches of Christ for many decades that the New Testament, properly understood, prohibited women from teaching or preaching to a mixed-gender assembly. Within the last half-century, however, there has once again been much study and discussion (and debate) of the issue. During the 1960s and 1970s, some congregations began employing women in formal ministry positions, often in children's ministries or in campus ministries (in which capacity they would work closely with female students). By the 1980s and 1990s, a few congregations had gone further, offering some opportunities for women to preach to the entire assembly, though this was, and remains, a relatively rare occurrence. Also indicative of change, or at least conversation, on this topic have been the various debates and public forums which have been held in the last few decades, as well as recent adjustments in university chapel policies. Today, a slight majority of the colleges and universities associated with Churches of Christ allow women to serve in some capacity during chapel services, though other schools still restrict those roles to male students.[16]

16. Steve Gardner, "Most Church-of-Christ Colleges No Longer Exclude Women From Leading in Worship Services: A List of Schools and Their Approach to Chapel," *Authentic Theology*, May 9, 2018, https://authentictheology.com/2018/05/09/most-church-of-christ-colleges-no-longer-exclude-women-from-leading-in-worship-services-a-list-of-schools-and-their-approach-to-chapel/.

Discussion Questions

1. Did you know that the issue of women serving in formal leadership roles had such a long (and in some ways, complex) history within Churches of Christ?

2. What can we gain from reading the stories of women like Nancy Gove Cram? Are there larger lessons that we can learn from their lives?

3. Do you see signs that Churches of Christ today are reconsidering their position on women's roles in congregational leadership? If so, in what ways?

APPENDIX:
RESOURCES USED AND OTHER
SUGGESTED READINGS

Given the small size of this book and the large amount of excellent scholarship on the history of Churches of Christ, any list of works that might be helpful for readers hoping to continue their studies now that this book is over will, of necessity, be incomplete. Nevertheless, especially in light of the lack of direct citations in the text of this work itself, I hope in this short essay to give a sense of the books and articles which have proved helpful to me in the writing of this book and/or in the concurrent writing of my dissertation.

Though it is now more than twenty years old, Richard T. Hughes's *Reviving the Ancient Faith: The Story of Churches of Christ in America* (William B. Eerdmans Publishing Company, 1996) remains the best single-volume introduction to our fellowship's history. Readers seeking a thorough overview of the Stone-Campbell

Movement writ large will likewise benefit from *The Stone-Campbell Movement: A Global History* (Chalice Press, 2013), edited by D. Newell Williams, Douglas A. Foster, and Paul M. Blowers. Another reference work edited by the same trio, along with the late Anthony L. Dunnavant, that should be on the shelf of any movement historian is *The Encyclopedia of the Stone-Campbell Movement* (Eerdmans, 2004).

A number of older works on the history of Churches of Christ remain immensely useful as well. Earl West's four-volume *The Search for the Ancient Order: A History of the Restoration Movement* (Religious Book Service, 1949-1987) revolutionized the field by placing Churches of Christ, not the Disciples, at the center of the larger movement's history. David Edwin Harrell Jr.'s two-volume *A Social History of the Disciples of Christ* (reprint, University of Alabama, 2003), paired with his *The Churches of Christ in the Twentieth Century: Homer Hailey's Personal Journey of Faith* (University of Alabama, 2000) reminds us that our fellowship has not existed in a vacuum but has been impacted by larger sociological forces shaping our society. (The latter volume is also the standard history of the non-institutional Churches of Christ, of which Harrell is himself a member.) A much more recent work of great import is James L. Gorman's *Among the Early Evangelicals: The Transatlantic Origins of the Stone-Campbell Movement*

(Abilene Christian University Press, 2017), which challenges the insights contained within an older, though still useful, work by Nathan O. Hatch called *The Democratization of American Christianity* (Yale University Press, 1989).

There are several good works on the history of the Christadelphians, though there has been relatively little exchange between scholars of that group and scholars of the Stone-Campbell Movement as a whole. Two now-out-of-print books may be the most thorough, if not accessible, points of entry. Bryan R. Wilson's *Sects and Society: A Sociological Study of Three Religious Groups in Britain* (reprint, Greenwood Press, Inc., 1978) recounts the story of the British Christadelphians, while Charles H. Lippy's *The Christadelphians in North America* (The Edwin Mellen Press, 1989) does the same for those on the other side of the pond. My own forthcoming article on Christadelphian theology in the *Stone-Campbell Journal*, though shorter, will likely be easier to track down, as are David Lertis Matson's two articles on the formerly anonymous Christadelphian woman who challenged Alexander Campbell's teachings on rebaptism (*Stone-Campbell Journal* 11:1, Spring 2008; *Stone-Campbell Journal* 14:2, Fall 2011).

Likewise, two books on the history of the International Churches of Christ, both by group members, are of great value if one can find affordable copies. C. Foster

Stanback's *Into All Nations: A History of the International Churches of Christ* (Illumination Publishers International, 2005) is a traditional denominational history, while Thomas A. Jones's *In Search of a City: An Autobiographical Perspective on a Remarkable but Controversial Movement* (DPI Books, 2007) offers a more personal take on the group. John F. Wilson's brief overview of ICOC history in a special issue of *Leaven* (18:2, 2010) is available freely online and is also a helpful resource.

Few, if any, scholars have contributed as much to the recovery of the story of black Churches of Christ as Edward J. Robinson, whose academic biographies (*To Save My Race From Abuse: The Life of Samuel Robert Cassius*, University of Alabama, 2007; *Show Us How You Do It: Marshall Keeble and the Rise of Black Churches of Christ in the United States, 1914-1968*, University of Alabama, 2008) provided me accessible avenues into the history of this rich tradition. Wes Crawford's *Shattering the Illusion: How African American Churches of Christ Moved from Segregation to Independence* (Abilene Christian University, 2013) tells the sad story of the end of the Nashville Christian Institute and its impact on race relations within our fellowship, while *Reconciliation Reconsidered: Advancing the National Conversation on Race in Churches of Christ* (Abilene Christian University, 2016), edited by Tanya Smith

Brice, is recommended reading for all persons troubled by the state of the relationship between predominantly white and predominantly black Churches of Christ today.

Readers interested in learning more about the history and roles of women in Churches of Christ will also do well to start with a pair of more biographically focused works. Loretta Long (Hunnicutt)'s *The Life of Selina Campbell: A Fellow Soldier in the Cause of Restoration* (University of Alabama, 2001) profiles the wife of prominent restoration figure Alexander Campbell. Bonnie Miller's *Messengers of the Risen Son in the Land of the Rising Sun: Single Women Missionaries in Japan* (Leafwood Publishers, 2008) recounts the stories of those women who took it upon themselves to share the gospel in Japan in the pre-World War Two era. Lastly, D'Esta Love's edited collection *Finding Their Voices: Sermons by Women in the Churches of Christ* (Abilene Christian University, 2015) contains the texts of those sermons along with a helpful historical overview written by the editor.

INDEX

Abilene Christian College (University), 71, 80

Alabama Christian College (Faulkner University), 60

American Bible Society (ABS), 12

American Christian Missionary Society (ACMS), 24–25, 27, 35, 38, 98

American Christian Review, 38, 43–44

Anderson, Louisa, 96

Apostolic Advocate, 30

Baptism, 14, 16, 20, 30, 96

Bevis, Jim, 72

Bible Chair Journal, 71

Boll, R.H., 54–56

Boston Movement, 73, 77–81

Bowser, George Philip (G.P.), 91–92

Campbell, Alexander, xii, 11, 13–17, 19–21, 25, 29–31, 37–38, 46, 53, 59, 96–98

Campbell, Thomas, xi–xii, 11, 13–15, 17, 19–21

Campus Evangelism, 72, 75–76

Cane Ridge, 13

Chalk, John Allen, 72

Christadelphians 30–31, 96

Christian Association of Washington, 15, 20

Christian Baptist, 15

Christian Church, 7, 20, 46

Christian Connexion, 97

Christian Echo, 91

Christian Magazine, 28

Christian Messenger, 14

Christian Standard, 38

"Christians only," 13, 97

Church, Samuel, 29

Civil War, 19, 27, 30, 32, 35, 37–38, 44, 89

Cogdill, Roy, 62–63

Contending for the Faith, 70

Cornyn, John, 87

Cotton, John, 6–7

Cox, John D., 64

Cram, Nancy Gove, 97–98, 101

Crossroads movement, xii, 76–77, 79

Disciples of Christ, xii, 20, 44–47, 49, 51, 69, 91, 98,

Disciples Divinity House, 40

Duck Dynasty, 86

Elpis Israel, 31

Emerson, Ralph Waldo, 19

Errett, Isaac, 38–39

Fanning, Tolbert, 25

Ferguson, Jesse B., xii, 27–29, 31, 33

First Amendment, 11

Florida Christian College (Florida College), 60, 64

Forrester, George, 16

Franklin, Benjamin, 22, 38

Freed-Hardeman College (University), 70, 76, 85

Garfield, James A., xii, 36–37, 40–41, 43–44, 49, 69, 86

Garrett, Leroy, 69

Goodpasture, B.C., 63–64

Gospel Advocate, 35, 38, 46, 54, 63, 68, 85, 99

Gospel Guardian, 62–63

Gray, Fred, 87, 92

Hardeman, N.B., 63

Harding College (University), 60

Harrell, Ed, 70

Harrell, Pat, 69

Herald of Truth, 60

Highland Church of Christ (Abilene, Texas), 60

Hogan, Richard Nathaniel (R.N.), 91

Holman, Silena, 99

Holt, Lester, 87

Holy Spirit, 7, 16, 20, 76, *baptism of*, 97

Hoover, J. Edgar, 68

Instrumental music, 22–23, 25, 27, 32, 39, 47–48, 72, 98

Integrity, 70

International Christian Church, 81

International Churches of Christ (ICOC), 75, 79–81, 83

Jones, Abner, 13

Keeble, Marshall, 91–92

Kennedy, John F., 68

Ketcherside, Carl, 69

Kriete, Henry, 80

Lard, Moses, 23

Larimore, Theophilus Brown (T.B.), vii, 47–48

Lipscomb, David, xii, 25, 36, 38, 44, 46, 68, 99

Lucado, Max, 85–86

Lucas, Chuck, 76–78

Malherbe, Abraham, 69

McKean, Kip, 77–81

Millennialism, xii, 48, 51–57, 59, 62

Mission, 70

Muscle and a Shovel, 4

Nashville Bible School, 48

Nation, Carrie, 97–99

New Hermeneutic, 84

O'Kelly, James, 13, 21

Owen, Robert, 21

Pentecost (Day of), 4, 5, 8

Pepperdine College (University), 60, 85, 93

Purcell, John, 22

Reagan, Wesley, 72
Restoration Quarterly, 69
Rice, Ira Y., Jr., 70
Richardson, Robert, 16
Rowe, John F., 43
Scott, Walter, xii, 5, 11, 13–14,
    16–17, 19
Sewell, Jesse P., 71
Slavery, 32, 35, 89
Smith, Elias, 13
Smith, Joseph, 13
Society(ies), 22, 24, 32, 35, 38–
    40, 62
Sold-Out Discipling Move-
    ment, 81
Southeastern Institute of the
    Bible (Heritage Christian
    University), 93
Southwestern Christian Col-
    lege, 93
Spiritual Sword, 70
Springfield Presbytery, 14
Stone, Barton W.,xii, 7, 13–
    17, 19, 21, 31, 46, 98
Stone-Campbell Movement
    (Restoration Movement),
    xii, 21, 35, 95, 97
Synod of Kentucky, 14
Synod of North America, 15
Tant, Fanning Yater, 62–63
Tant, J.D., 63
Taylor, Preston, 90
Terrell, Melissa Garrett, 97
*The Way of the Churches of
    Christ in New England*, 6
Thomas, John, xii, 29–31, 33,
    96

Thoreau, Henry David, 19
Vermillion, Rex, 72
Vietnam War, 68
Wallace, Cled, 63
Wallace, Foy E., Jr., 55–56,
    63–64
Warren, Thomas B., 70
Wineskins, 85
Word and Work, 56
Yankovic, "Weird Al," 86
Young, C.B.F., 63

CPSIA information can be obtained
at www.ICGtesting.com
Printed in the USA
BVHW061722071019
560431BV00007B/370/P

9 781732 048348